· THE ANGEL INSIDE ·

· THE ·
ANGEL INSIDE

*Michelangelo's Secrets for
Following Your Passion and Finding
the Work You Love*

CHRIS WIDENER

BROADWAY BOOKS

New York

BROADWAY

Copyright © 2004 by Chris Widener

Published in the United States by Broadway Books,
an imprint of the Crown Publishing Group,
a division of Random House, Inc., New York.
www.crownpublishing.com

BROADWAY BOOKS and the Broadway Books colophon are
trademarks of Random House, Inc.

Originally published in slightly different form by
YourSuccessStore.com. Subsequently published in hardcover in the
United States by Doubleday, a division of Random House, Inc.,
New York, in 2007.

Library of Congress Cataloging-in-Publication Data
Widener, Chris.
The Angel inside : Michelangelo's secrets for following your passion
and finding the work you love / by Chris Widener. — 1st ed.
p.   cm.
Originally published in 2004 by YourSuccessStore.com.
Includes index.
1. Vocational guidance. 2. Career development. I. Title.
HF5381.W54 2007
650.14—dc22   2006031858

ISBN 978-0-307-71953-9

Printed in the United States of America

Design by Jennifer Ann Daddio

3 5 7 9 10 8 6 4 2

*To Lisa, Christopher,
Hannah, Rebekah, and
Sarah—My Angels!*

FOREWORD

Sometimes fiction is truer than fact.

Good fiction doesn't just entertain—it also educates. That is the case with *The Angel Inside*. Chris Widener has wrapped truth in a fictional story that engages our interest while educating our intellect and encouraging our heart.

I've been fortunate enough to see the *David* in person while visiting Florence. Photographs and verbal descriptions don't capture the magnificence of the sculpture Michelangelo so masterfully created.

The *David* is housed in a museum within a large, bustling city. The people who live there or visit comprise the spectrum of human experience. Some are highly educated, while others have limited formal education; some are unbelievably wealthy, while others barely manage to scrape by. Some live their lives large, while others live lives more circumscribed by circumstance.

I believe that the *David* reminds us of what each of our lives can be, regardless of what they are today. It is an ideal of beauty and perfection that inspires us to aspire to greater beauty in our own lives.

Perhaps the simple truths we learn in *The Angel Inside* are so appealing because we live in a complex world. We are anxiously searching for the essence, the foundation, that will help us build our own successful lives and businesses.

I agree with Chris: There is a masterpiece within each of us, waiting to emerge. Unfortunately, not all of us understand our potential or how to achieve it. After reading *The Angel Inside*, I believe you'll better realize the God-given potential you possess, to help make your life the masterpiece it is meant to be.

—Mark Sanborn

· THE ANGEL INSIDE ·

FINDING THE ANGEL INSIDE YOU

*Every person has this tremendous capacity
to be both king and warrior, a person
of value and a person of accomplishment—
of beauty and power.*

Tom Cook had come to Europe looking for direction, but with only one day left on his trip he was reluctantly coming to the conclusion that it may have evaded his grasp. Feeling frustrated with the way things were going at work and at home, he had planned a two-week "getaway" vacation that he hoped would clear his head and give him the opportunity to do some soul-searching. Ultimately, he believed that his time away from the United States would relieve the pressure he felt at work and allow him to make some thoughtful decisions about his future. He had already been to England, France, and Spain, but had yet to gain any real clarity about himself or where his career was headed. He was still as confused as he'd been the day he flew out of JFK. Today was his third and final day in Florence, Italy, the last city on his itinerary—and his time there was almost gone. But then, something happened . . .

Florence. Firenze. City of romance, art, food, and wine. Most who go there are overwhelmed by its beauty. The greatest masterpieces in the world can be found in its museums. Some of the most famous, creative, and influential names in history were born and made their lives here. It is, in all its glory, a cultural hub of history and art beyond comparison. Tom had imagined it would be the perfect place to find direction, joy, and inspiration.

It was early afternoon and he was sitting on a bench in a bustling plaza. He was tired. Tired of traveling. Tired of searching. Tired of life. Just tired.

As he sat with his heavy backpack on the ground at his feet, Tom watched a vast sea of people coming and going, running around just as they did back home. Some of the people seemed happy, others looked like they were in a frenzy to be somewhere else, while still others walked along with their love, gazing into each other's eyes. But all Tom saw was a sea of people that brought more questions than answers. *Where are they going? What do they look forward to? Are they really happy?* He hated to admit it, but he was a cynic at thirty. He certainly wasn't happy, and couldn't imagine that anyone else could be either. Life just didn't work that way.

As he sat, his head slowly drifted downward into his hands as he lost eye contact with the crowd around him. He was among many but was somehow still alone. Then, just as he was feeling sorry for himself, a voice spoke.

"My, my. You look much too young and handsome to be so sad of heart," the voice said.

Tom looked up—barely—to see who had interrupted his self-pity. It was an old man. Out of courtesy, he slowly raised his head, still not saying anything. His eyes locked on the old man, surveying him. The old man was an exercise in contrast. On one hand, he looked . . . rough. On the other hand, he had an elegant air about him. He was old, that was for sure. Seventy, maybe? Seventy-five? His unruly dark brown hair and scruffy beard looked ready for a trip to the barber. Medium height, thin, but with large biceps and pillar-like forearms that seemed out of place on the old man's body. His craggy face and calloused hands had a blue-collar look about them. But the old man's clothes revealed the taste of a connoisseur; you could tell he wasn't buying off the rack at the corner store. This was a man who knew a tailor or two. An expensive beret topped his head, and wild as it was, his hair peeked out from underneath with an artistic flair. He wore a beautifully patterned silk shirt that flowed down to the top of natty slacks. His leather shoes were impeccable.

The old man spoke again. "Yes, you are sad. I can tell." He didn't ask permission before sitting down next to Tom. Tom couldn't believe this was happening. He was still caught up in being alone and depressed. "But I can also see that you certainly have much to be happy about. Tell me, what is your name?"

"Tom."

"Tom? Tom . . . Thomas?"

"Yes, Thomas."

"Ah, yes, I see. Like the doubter?" the old man grinned. "You are doubting, aren't you? Doubting Thomas. What are you doubting, Thomas?"

Tom thought, *What am I doubting? This is crazy. I have a crazy Italian sitting next to me.* Finally he said, "Well, I appreciate your concern, but I am not really doubting anything."

"Pardon me, Thomas. I know you must find this intrusive, but I have intuition for these kinds of things. I have been around now for a very long time. I have seen much. I see that you are doubting. But perhaps you do not like that word. Well, then, what is it that burdens you this day, Thomas?"

Tom decided to humor the old man. What could it hurt? After all, things couldn't get worse. "Well, let's see. I just turned thirty and I am nowhere near where I want to be in my career. My boss thinks I have zero career potential—at least it sure comes across that way because he keeps sticking me with jobs that no one else wants. My job seems like a treadmill that will never get me to where I want to go. My girlfriend just dumped me because I don't have enough 'upside,' as she calls it. Even my parents wonder when I am going to begin to make something of myself. Frankly, I am beginning to believe I'm useless."

A young couple walked by and asked the old man if he would take their picture. He obliged, and they quickly posed for him. When he was finished he returned their camera and they bounded down the street, laughing giddily.

The old man turned back to Thomas. "Useless, I see," said the old man. "That does sound disheartening. I can see why you would be sad, even in this beautiful city. Most people here—especially the tourists—are happy." He paused and then asked, "How long have you been in Florence?"

"This is my third day."

"Three days. That is wonderful! When do you depart?"

"Tomorrow morning at six-thirty."

"Oh. Not much time left then. Have you taken in any of the art?" the old man then asked.

"Sure," Tom replied. "I took a quick tour. What would a trip to Florence be without seeing the art, right?"

"You make a very good point, young Thomas. I myself think that the art is the most important reason to come to Florence. I assume, then, that you saw Michelangelo's work the *David—Il Gigante*, as they call it—The Giant?"

"Yeah, sure. That's one of the biggies, right? No pun intended."

"Yes, it is. The biggest in my opinion. And tell me, Thomas, what did you learn from the *David*?"

"Learn? Uh, I didn't *learn* anything. I saw it. He was huge. Naked. It was great. I left."

"Oh my, you didn't learn anything from *Il Gigante*?" The old man looked at his watch. "It is one o'clock. Come now, we haven't much time." The old man began to stand as he said this.

Thomas looked up. "Come where? For what?" He was perfectly happy sitting right where he was. Now this old wannabe sage wanted to drag him off on an unscheduled tour.

"To go see *Il Gigante*, of course! There is so much to learn from him and from Michelangelo. Come, you will see."

Okay, this is crazy. But the old man had an endearing quality about him. He was harmless, and besides, what else would Tom do for the rest of the afternoon other than watch birds land on the heads of statues?

Tom stood up and grabbed his backpack. "Okay. I'm game. Let's go."

The old man beamed broadly. "Fantastic, Thomas." He put one arm around Tom and then said something that took Tom aback. *"This day will change your life forever."*

With this, they began their journey to the foot of *Il Gigante* in the Galleria dell'Accademia. They made their way through the city walking at a fast pace. *This old guy can really move!* "Excuse me, can we slow down a bit? This backpack is kind of heavy."

The old man barely turned back as he said, "Of course, pardon me. I am just excited to have you see *Il Gigante* again." Yet his pace slowed down very little . . .

Down the street, across a bridge, a right turn and then a left. Tom hadn't thought it was so far away. The old man took him through an open market, where he paused just long enough to buy some bread from a merchant he obviously knew. He broke it in half and handed a piece to Tom. "Enjoy!" he said as he headed off again. Tom wished he could stay and bask in the aroma of the baked goods. That had been his favorite part of Florence—the smells of the wine, the cheese, the bread, and the fruit. *I should have eaten a bigger lunch.* Every now and then the old man would say hello to someone or pat someone on the back as they went by.

Finally, they arrived at the Galleria dell'Accademia, skirting the line and going directly to the entrance. The women in the ticket office seemed to know the old man and waved them on. Tom had been here a couple of days ago. As he had mentioned to the old man, he had come because that's what tourists do when they come to Florence—they look in awe at the *David*. Somehow it hadn't struck him as awesome when he had come before. This time was different though. It seemed . . . *otherworldly*. It was a strange feeling. This time he noticed the soaring ceiling, the beauty of the room, and the sound of the hollowness of the space. People spoke little in the presence of the *David*.

They just looked at the statue for a moment, then the old man said with a sense of wonder, "Isn't it beautiful? Just grand!"

"It's *big*, that's for sure."

"Yes! It really is a giant: thirteen and a half feet tall. It took Michelangelo twenty-eight months to sculpt him from beginning to end!"

They stood silently. Tom thought that the old man sure seemed to be enjoying himself. He was looking at the statue like a proud father. It seemed kind of weird to Tom, who thought to himself, *Well, we're in the classroom. I wonder when class begins?*

After what seemed like an eternity, the old man said, "Thomas, do you wonder why I brought you here?"

"Sure. The thought crossed my mind. I mean, *David* is great and all, and I know Michelangelo was one of the greatest artists of all time, but what does that have to do with me?"

"Very good question, Thomas. I have an answer. But first another question: What do you know about Michelangelo?"

"Let's see. He was Italian."

The old man laughed. "Yes, that he was."

"Other than that, he lived in the late fourteen hundreds and early fifteen hundreds."

"Yes. He died in 1564. It is more accurate to say the mid–fifteen hundreds. What else?"

"He was an incredible artist who painted and sculpted."

"That's correct. Do you know what he painted and sculpted?"

"All I know is the *David* and the Sistine Chapel. Right?"

"Yes, those as well as many others. Is there anything else you know about Michelangelo and *Il Gigante*?"

"Nope. That about covers it."

"I see." The old man paused to think. "Then we are ready to begin."

"All right." Tom could hardly imagine how this was going to go.

"Let us start with a story: One day, Michelangelo was working on this marble that would become *David*, and a young child came by where he was working. The young boy asked Michelangelo why he was working so hard hitting the rock. Michelangelo said to him, 'Young boy, there is an angel inside of this rock and I am setting him free.'"

He let the story sink in. "Do you see the point of that story, Thomas?"

Tom looked at the *David* and thought. After running the possibilities through his mind he said, "I would guess that he meant that he was trying to make something beautiful out of the marble."

"You are on the right track, Thomas. But there is more."

"How so?"

"Let me explain. In essence, you are correct. But there is more to it than meets the eye. Things specific to you; things that will mean something for you—for everyone, really."

"I'm all ears."

"Thomas, what do those who are closest to you think of you?"

"I think they like me." He then corrected himself. "They love me. But . . ." Tom drifted off and looked away.

"Yes?" the old man probed.

"They don't think much of what I have done with my life, or what I'm doing, or for that matter what I'm capable of. They think of me as your basic loser, I guess."

"What do you mean, exactly?" the old man asked.

"They just have certain ideas about what being successful means, what I should be doing, how much money I should be making, what class of people I should be with. Things like that. Things that I am not."

"Hmmm. That must be painful, yes?"

"Yes." It was quite painful, in fact. Tom hadn't expected to be psychoanalyzed.

"Let me give you the history of that big piece of marble. That marble was originally cut for work before Michelangelo was even born. In fact, it was commissioned to Agostino di Duccio in 1464—eleven years before Michelangelo came into this world. But Agostino could not decide what to do with it, so he gave up the commission. Then, in 1476, when Michelangelo was just one year old, another artist by the name of Antonio Rossellino was commissioned to work with the marble. As with Agostino, he could not see what the marble could become. Even Leonardo da Vinci was asked to consider working the marble. He declined for two reasons. First, he thought sculpting was a low form of art. He was arrogant that way. Brilliant but arrogant." The old man rolled his eyes as if disgusted. "Second, he too could not see what that marble could become. Three artists—one of them one of the most famous ever—came before Michelangelo and could not see what that marble held deep inside. But Michelangelo, he saw the angel deep at rest within the rock, waiting to be set free to inspire Florence and the world!"

"Thomas, do you see what I am trying to teach you?"

"Sort of. I mean, those other guys were all great, beyond great, at what they did. But even they couldn't see the potential of what the marble could become . . . Is that what you mean?" Now Tom was leaning toward the statue, his hand on his chin.

"That is part of it, yes. But there is more. It is true that they could not see what that rock could become. But Michelangelo's words carry a deeper meaning. Do you understand?"

"I'm afraid I don't."

"Thomas, there is an angel inside *you*. There is a person of *beauty*. There is a person of *power*. *David* represented both. If you remember, the real David—the onetime King of Israel—was a very diverse fellow. Not many men have interests that range from writing poetry and playing the harp to slaying giants and going to war. David, both the man and the statue, was beautiful *and* powerful. There is a lesson there for all people. We all have a beauty to us. We are valuable just for who we are. But we are also capable of tremendous power. We can become people of great accomplishment. We can face the giants in our lives, even as David did, and win." The old man looked at Tom to see if he was getting it. The old man could tell that he was beginning to, but suspected Tom still had doubts that he could be or do something special.

Despite his skepticism, Tom wanted to hear more. "Keep going," he said.

"Think of the rejection of that marble. David lay there since the beginning of time. Many people looked at it and saw *nothing*. Nothing! No potential. 'The marble was cut too thin,' many people said. But Michelangelo had the *vision* for what it could become." The old man began to turn the corner on his idea. "Do you know much about the story of the real David, Thomas?"

"Less than I know about Michelangelo." Tom grinned.

"This is okay. You will learn today—*and it will change your life forever.* Let me tell you an ancient story from the life of the real David: There was a prophet named Samuel. God Himself told Samuel that he would find the next king in the home of a man named Jesse. So Samuel went to Jesse and told him this. Then he asked Jesse to allow him to see his sons. Jesse promptly called them together and lined them up. One by one Samuel went down the line dismissing each son. When he got to the end he was a bit confused. He asked if there were any other sons. Jesse said there was one other, but it could not possibly be him. He was only a shepherd, a tender of sheep. Samuel asked Jesse for his name. Jesse's answer: *David*. Jesse sent for David, and he was brought before Samuel. Samuel knew immediately that this was the next king. Jesse could not believe it—and David's brothers did not want to.

"Explaining this to Jesse, Samuel spoke a profound truth: 'Man looks on the outside, but God, He looks on the inside.' "

"That's a great story," said Tom.

"Yes, this is incredible, Thomas. This is the first truth that you must realize in becoming the person you desire to become. No matter what you think your life looks like now, or what you think your father thinks, there is an angel that lies dormant within you. Every person has this tremendous capacity to be both king and warrior, a person of value and a person of accomplishment—of beauty and power. When you understand this, when you embrace it and come to truly believe it, it will change your life forever. Your entire destiny will open before you."

"I get it in concept, but how can I believe it for myself? I mean, there are no signs of it anywhere in my life."

"Thomas, you do not look far enough. You must search for this deep within. Sometimes you must dwell on this truth for quite some time, every day reminding yourself of it, and then one day it becomes yours. You finally believe it. But there is a way to foster this belief. Let me ask you: What are you good at? Everyone has something that they are good at. When you know this, it will suggest what your angel will look like."

"Believe it or not, I have always had a creative streak. When I was a kid, I was always dreaming up stories to tell to my friends and relatives, putting on silly little plays, writing stories, and stuff like that. I've just never pursued it much."

"Very good then. You are a creator. This is a beautiful gift that you have. How do you use this in your work, Thomas?"

"That's the point. I don't. I got my MBA—Masters of Business Administration—and went to work for a Fortune 500 company in their mergers and acquisitions department. I crunch numbers and evaluate business plans. Then I hand my analyses up the pipe to people who make the decisions. I'm a cog in the wheel of commerce." Tom leaned back, looked up, and sighed a sigh of desperation . . . or resignation.

"Tell me, how did you end up in this business?"

"Take a guess: my dad. He's the CEO of a major corporation, makes a few million bucks a year, and flies in the corporate jet. He pushed me into it. It seems like since the third grade I was being told, 'Tom, this world isn't going to hand you anything. You have to take whatever you want. The way to get what you want is to make money. And the way to make money is in big business. Tom,' he would say, 'here is the Golden Rule: He who has the gold makes the rules.' For years I really thought that was the Golden Rule!"

"And so you pursued money?"

"I pursued business because that's where my dad led me to believe the money was. I thought it would make him happy and proud of me."

"Thomas, I do not know you well, yet I know many young people *like* you. You have yet to see what angel is inside you. The outer shell has yet to come off so that you and the world can see what beauty lies beneath. You have yet to fully display your inner value and worth. Before you can do so, you must commit to this and begin your search for the angel inside you."

Tom stood silently, trying to internalize the truths the old man was speaking about. In theory he believed it, but he just couldn't see it in his own life. He had spent so many years trying to become the person others wanted him to be that he wondered if he would ever be able to find the true self that was below the surface.

After a few moments, the old man spoke. "You will not find the answers in one afternoon, Thomas. Yet I tell you so that the seed of this thought can be planted inside you. In time it will grow to become a driving force in your life. Now, you have learned the first lesson: No matter what others may say, there is an angel inside you, waiting to be set free. In time, you will find that angel and let him soar."

"I wish somebody would tell my dad that," Tom said.

"Maybe *you* should."

2

THE POWER
OF FOLLOWING
YOUR PASSION

*There comes a time in every person's life
when they must decide whether they will follow
what they want for their life or
what someone else wants for their life.*

"Thomas, this brings us to the second lesson you
must learn from *Il Gigante*..." The old man then
paused, his face deep in thought.

"And that is...?" Tom asked.

"Imagine if the *David* had never been sculpted.
Or the Sistine Chapel painted. Two of the world's

greatest works of art, loved and admired by people all throughout the world." The old man was waving his hands; as he leaned closer he spoke quietly. "Now listen closely, Thomas. None of this would have been possible had Michelangelo followed his father's wishes." He turned and looked again at the *David*.

"I don't get it. What do you mean? What were his father's wishes?"

The old man breathed deeply. "This is very important for you, as it was for Michelangelo. Again, a story: Lodovico was the name of Michelangelo's father. He was a good man—a minor official in Florence. He owned some properties and had some money, but as he grew older he saw his wealth diminishing. His hope was that his children would restore the family name to its glory. He wanted his children to earn money, own property, and befriend the ruling class. As for Michelangelo, he wanted him to own a business or two, to become a merchant who would be respected in Florence. But, just like you, Thomas, young Michelangelo had other ideas."

"How old was Michelangelo when this happened?"

"It started when he was a young boy. At thirteen he began as an apprentice for Domenico Ghirlandaio, a well-known painter. This, however, infuriated Lodovico. This was not at all the path that he wanted for his boy. They argued much of the time. Lodovico did what he could to stop Michelangelo. He thought that being an artist was of the lower class."

"So what happened? I mean, I know the end of the story, but what made Michelangelo go ahead anyway?"

The old man turned to Tom and lifted his left hand in the air, raising his index finger to make a point. "This, Thomas, is the second lesson *and it will change your life forever.*"

He certainly has a flair for the dramatic, Tom thought.

"Listen closely: No matter what others think you should do or become, *you must always follow your passion, and your passion only.* This is what Michelangelo did. He turned away from his father. He found a mentor. He apprenticed himself to Ghirlandaio and began to learn the art. Soon after, when even Ghirlandaio knew that Michelangelo was something special, Michelangelo moved into the home of Lorenzo di Medici, of *the* Medicis—the most powerful people in all of Florence. Lorenzo was a patron of the arts and he put his hand upon young Michelangelo. This was very fortunate for Michelangelo!"

"What did Loda . . . Lovi . . ."

"Lodovico."

"Michelangelo's dad. What did he do?"

"There was nothing he could do. Michelangelo was

pursuing his passion. It wasn't until after Michelangelo made his mark that Lodovico reluctantly gave his approval. Think for a moment, Thomas. What would happen if you simply quit what you are doing and began to do something that you love, something that burns in your heart—your *passion*?"

"My dad would kill me," Tom deadpanned.

"No, of course he would not. What would really be the problem, Thomas? Think. The answer is right there."

"He would think poorly of me." Tom looked down as he said it.

"From what you tell me, this is most likely true. He would think poorly of you. And this is exactly why your angel is still lying inside of the rock instead of standing as the warrior king. This is why you are frustrated; this is why your heart aches."

"So what do I do? I'm thirty years old. My father has spent hundreds of thousands of dollars on my education to make me a businessman. With all due respect, I'm not a thirteen-year-old prodigy in fifteenth-century Italy."

"And with all due respect, young Thomas, you are not much of a businessman either, are you?" *Ouch*, Tom thought. That one hurt, but it was just a flesh wound. The old man smiled. "You are not a good businessman only because it is not in your heart to be a businessman. There is no passion there. As you have said yourself, you are a creative person. You need a job that allows you to express that creativity. 'Crunching numbers,' as you put it, doesn't allow you that."

"Okay, but again—What do I *do*? Theory only goes so far."

"You quit. Or at least you begin the process of moving away from what you are doing to what you want to be doing. You are young and without responsibilities—you have no family—so it would be easier for you. An older man with a wife and children, I would encourage to move more slowly, but I would still encourage him to move. You, though, could quit soon—especially after you learn a few more lessons about how to create the life you desire."

"Quit my job? That's impossible."

"It is not possible, or it would not be enjoyable? There is a big difference between the two."

"Go on."

"Thomas, the world is filled with people who do not do what they love. Most people drift through life like a feather in the wind. They do not have a purpose that comes from their passion, from their strength. These are the men and women who your philosopher Thoreau said lead 'lives of quiet desperation.' Time passes, and as they near death, all they are left with is regret. Yet there is nothing they can do about it. Their lives are lost because they did not decide to do what they wanted. Thomas, the worst thing that can happen to you is that your father may be disappointed in you, correct?"

"Yeah, I think that's as far as it would go. I don't think he would disown me or anything like that."

"My question for you: Do you think your father is disappointed in you now?"

A long silence followed, then Tom admitted, "Yes. I'm sure he is." He hated to say it. His whole life had been devoted to pleasing his father. This larger-than-life man, so successful in everything he did, towered over his life. His father had been a 4.0 student and the quarterback of his football team; he'd gone to Harvard on a full academic scholarship, then Harvard Business School before conquering the world of business. Tom had tried, but he had failed to live up to what his father wanted him to be. Part of him wanted to weep aloud right there. Another part felt free. He was beginning to be honest with himself.

"Yes, I am sure he is, Thomas. He most likely is. Because you will never be successful doing what you do not want to do. You will certainly sabotage yourself."

"I know what you're saying. I've been dreading work so much lately that I've been getting in late pretty much every day, surfing the Web when I should be putting together reports. I know I'm only hurting myself, but I guess part of me is rebelling against this job because it's what my dad wanted—not me."

"It is good that you recognize this, Thomas. Here is something else you should realize. Your father may always be disappointed in you, and there is nothing you can do about that, *but if you do not follow your passion, you will always be unhappy*. Of course, there is another way: You can make the hard decision to quit and begin to follow your passion. Yes, your father may be disappointed in you, but at least you will find passion in what you do—and your passion will lead to success."

"I guess I really can't control what my father will think, can I?"

"Indeed. Your father is just a man, Thomas. He was once a little boy and was shaped by his parents. They poured themselves into him and he did the same to you. Humans are by no means perfect, are they? If we do not watch ourselves, we pass along many hurtful things to our children. Your father believes that money is the standard for achievement. This is not true, and you know this.

"Thomas, there comes a time in every person's life when they must decide whether they will follow what they want for their life or what someone else wants for their life. There will be many voices that seek to influence you. Parents will pressure you, most of the time out of good intentions because they love you. Brothers and sisters will judge your decisions and look down on you. Friends will think less of you, and some may even leave you. But there is one truth that remains: *It is your life, not theirs.* What do you think of that?"

"I think I have been living my father's life, not mine."

"It sounds like you have. But it is not too late. You are only thirty years old. But even if you were sixty, it is never too late to change and live for your passion." The old man paused to let his words sink in and then continued, "Do you know what I find to be the most beautiful irony in this story of Michelangelo, Thomas?"

"What's that?"

"Lodovico was concerned most with money, image, and class, much like your father, and he did not want his son to do anything that would be considered to be of the lower class. Yet, in following his own passion, Michelangelo has set the standard and the very definition of class for *centuries*. His works of art are priceless. People travel from all over the world to see his work and gaze in wonder and awe at their exquisitely detailed beauty. By following his own passion, he was able to achieve what his father actually wanted: respect for the family name. Had he become a Florentine merchant, the world would never have known the name of Michelangelo."

Tom's mind was racing. He felt alive, or at least like he was coming alive. The possibility of doing something besides mergers and acquisitions thrilled him. It had never seemed an option before, and now it was as though it could actually become a reality. The old man's words echoed through his mind.

Yet he still had concerns. Changing careers seemed like a big leap—an exciting leap, but a big leap nonetheless. He thought about the way Michelangelo had apprenticed himself to Ghirlandaio, and realized that he too would need a mentor to help him make the transition, maybe even one who could use an extra pair of hands. That might make pursuing a new path more doable. He began to think of creative paths to pursue and of the people he knew who already did those things well, especially those who might be willing to mentor him.

"This day will forever change your life." He was beginning to believe that maybe, just maybe, the old man was right. Could a chance meeting on a park bench in a country halfway around the world become the turning point in his life? He looked at his watch. Three o'clock. They had

been in front of the *David* for close to two hours. It had seemed like minutes, and now he wanted to learn everything he could from the old man in what time remained.

"Okay," Tom said. "I'm pretty sure I have lessons one and two. What's next?"

"You are a fine student, Thomas. You learn quickly when you put your mind to it. The test will be if you remember these truths later and implement them."

"I will, don't worry. What's next?"

3

BEING CONFIDENT
IN YOUR STRENGTH

*If you are to be successful, you must find
self-confidence in the things that you do well,
and then pursue them.*

"It is time to take a closer look at *Il Gigante*," the
old man said as he walked toward the statue. "I
will teach you a few more things here, and then I
have somewhere else to take you."

Tom followed until they were standing directly in front of the *David*. He was amazed at the

size. He hadn't gotten as close the first time he came to see it.

"So what is the next lesson?" Tom asked.

"What do you see before you, Thomas?"

"I see . . . a statue."

"You are perceptive," the old man teased. "Let me be more direct: What is the mood of David?"

"The mood?"

"Yes, what do you see?"

Tom thought. "Can you give me some hints?" he asked.

"Very well. When in the battle with Goliath is the sculpture taken from?"

"I don't know."

"Before or after?" the old man prompted.

Tom looked the *David* over closely. Sling over the shoulder. Rock in his hand. Looking at something—Goliath—to the left. His brow furrowed in concentration. It became obvious. "Before. Right before."

"Yes."

"Okay, why is that important?"

"A little more history for you, Thomas. Traditionally, statues of David were done so as to reflect him immediately *after* the battle. This was usually done by sculpting Goliath's head, severed from his body, at the feet of David.

Michelangelo purposefully brought David to life just *before* he slew the giant. He did this because of the political situation at the time when he made the statue. Italy was not united. It was many fiefdoms and cities, like Florence, which constantly had to worry about attacking armies, large and small. Statues in that day were made for their beauty, of course, but they also served as powerful political statements. The statue of David was to be placed in a prominent place, the Palazzo Vecchio, to make a statement to the people of Florence and to anyone who would think of attacking. This is why I asked you what mood David was made to portray. Given this new understanding, what do you think David was meant to portray?"

Tom stared intently at the *David*. He couldn't get it. "I just don't know."

"Here are the words David spoke to Goliath just before he took the sling to him: 'I will strike you down and remove your head from you. And I will give the dead bodies of the army of the Philistines this day to the birds of the sky and the wild beasts of the earth.' Now, given that these are the words David spoke to this massive giant just moments from the time when he stands here before us, what would you say David was feeling?"

Tom looked at that brow of David's. Then he thought he had it. "Confidence. He felt confident."

"Thomas, you are learning. That is exactly right. Michelangelo wanted to portray confidence. The confidence that David felt before his battle was the same confidence he wanted Florence to show to those who thought of overthrowing it. He wanted Florence to say, 'If you attack, you will die.' "

"So the lesson is *confidence*?" Tom asked.

"The lesson is that in order to achieve what you want out of life, you must be confident. And as it relates to following your passions and utilizing your strengths, you must *demonstrate* self-confidence."

"Uh, what if you don't have self-confidence?"

"Tell me, Thomas, do you know what confidence means, literally?"

"No, what?"

"In the Latin, confidence literally means 'with faith.' So you see, self-confidence means you have faith in yourself."

"But what if you don't have faith in yourself?" Tom asked.

"You must have faith in some aspect of yourself. For instance, there are many things that I do not do well. However, there are many things that I excel at. It is in these that I put my confidence. The lesson is this: If you are to be successful, you must find self-confidence in the things that you do well, and then pursue them. As the *David* has shown visitors to Florence for so many hundreds of years, *the secret is that you too must stand confidently in whatever you do."*

"How do I do that?"

"When you go home, begin spending some time doing work that allows you to use your strengths. And though I have known you only a short time, I can see that your strengths are numerous. You are open to change and advice. You're a good student. You're eager to learn. By finding a job that allows you to draw upon these strengths, you will feel and become more confident. The reason you have no confidence now is because you are not good at what you do. So you are reminded, both consciously and subconsciously, every day, that you are not good at what you spend most of your day doing. This breeds doubt, fear, and, ultimately, despair. One must work in his or her strength. Confidence comes from this."

"Check. I got it."

"Good, then may we move on?"

"I would hope so," Tom said eagerly. The old man was right; he was truly enjoying his role as student in the old man's classroom.

4

BEAUTY
THROUGH DETAILS

*The masters, the ones who succeed tremendously
and set the standard for others,
are those who master the details.*

"Very well, then, notice something else about
David. I want you to walk around the statue as
many times as necessary to give thought to this:
Michelangelo's *David* is by far the most famous
statue of David, perhaps the most famous statue
in the history of the world. Tell me, then, with so

many *Davids*, why is it that this statue before you has come to be known as the most beautiful? What gives *this David* its beauty? Now just walk, look, and let the answer come to you. When it does come to you, you will have learned the fourth lesson of a powerful life." Tom was hesitant. "Go," the old man implored.

Tom took nearly ten minutes, studying the *David* from every angle. He would walk and then stop and look for a few minutes, then continue. Finally he came back to stand next to the old man. Just as he stopped, a security guard came up to the two of them.

The guard obviously knew the old man. "Another new student?" he asked the old man.

"Yes, and a very fine one at that."

The guard leaned in close to Tom. "Pay attention. You may not know it now, but this old man has helped more people than you could ever imagine. I have seen him take people, one at a time, through here for decades. I'm sure he has told you, '*Today your life will change forever.*' It's true, as you will see."

Then the guard turned to the old man again. "Keep up the good work. Set him straight." Then he was off to make his rounds.

"Good-bye," the old man said as the guard left.

Then he turned his attention back to the task at hand. "Well, Thomas, to what conclusion have you come after looking *Il Gigante* over so closely?"

Tom was staring at the *David*. "I just don't see it. I'm sorry. I'm missing something." He turned to the old man. "What is it?"

The old man smiled. "I will not give you the answer so easily, Thomas. Let me ask you this: How realistic do you consider *Il Gigante?*"

"Well, very realistic. It looks just like a person. Is that it?"

"That is the first part. There are many statues that look real from a distance, but when you get close you begin to see that the form is just made of marble. It ceases to be very realistic. Now look again, as closely as you can. Look at the statue to see just how closely it resembles the human form in its exactness. Go ahead," he said, as he gestured for Tom to circle the statue again.

When Tom had rounded *David* once again, the old man asked, "What is your conclusion now, Thomas?"

"It is very real."

"Yes? In what ways? Tell me what you see."

"The toes. The muscles in his legs. The tendons. The veins. His stomach and rib cage. His shoulders and arms look just like a man's. His jaw, his eyes, and his brow. And his hair. They all look real."

"Yes, Thomas. This is what set Michelangelo apart from all others. These are the *details*."

"The lesson is details?" Thomas asked.

"Not quite. The lesson is that *the beauty is in the details*."

"Okay . . . Go on," Tom said.

"All throughout life there are people who do work of various sorts. Most people do average work. Some people do above-average work. The masters, the ones who succeed tremendously and set the standard for others, are those who master the details. The thing that makes an otherwise typical statue something that men and women today know in every culture is the emphasis on the details. *Il Gigante* finds its *beauty in the details*."

"How exactly does this apply to me?" Tom asked.

"This applies to everyone, Thomas. No matter what work you do, you must put your hand to it with the goal of absolute excellence—and excellence comes from painstaking attention to the details. In Michelangelo's day, artists were given special opportunities to dissect human cadavers so they could learn to understand anatomy. Many joke that as magnificent as Michelangelo was, he must have crucified someone so as to know firsthand the details of what Christ on the cross would truly look like. While this obviously is not true, it *is* true that he did indeed spend time mastering the human form through dissection. He would work for hours to see how the body came together and to see how the many parts layered over one another. Then, when he would take the chisel to the marble, he would simply uncover what he had seen in the actual human body."

"Hmmm. Okay, so what about me?"

"The lesson, Thomas, is that when we are working in areas that we have no passion for, when there is no pleasure attached, it is natural for us to simply do whatever will get us by, producing work that is mediocre at best. We find our passion in what we love, in what brings us joy. We can spend hours on end on our passions and find that we easily lose track of time. Passionate work is when you wake up in the morning and cannot wait to get to it. When we are so engrossed in the details of the work that we find ourselves forgetting everything else. Michelangelo had this kind of passion for his work, and because of it he plunged himself into the details. He wanted every statue and painting to look as though it might suddenly spring to life—with a few exceptions that you will learn of in a moment. Tell me, Thomas, is this true for you? Do you ignore the details of your work because of your lack of passion for what it is that you do?"

"Well, I am working with numbers and financials so I have to be somewhat exact, but I confess that I find myself slacking off more than I'd like. It's tough enough just showing up every day, let alone doing any more work than I have to. So no, I do not have the 'beauty of the details,' as you put it."

"You see that this is all a progression, yes? Do you see that once you have the passion and the work you are good at, then you are able to create your own lasting masterpiece: A life that is beautiful and powerful? When you get home and begin to work at what you love, not only will you have the passion to master the details, you will for the first time in your life *be able to*. This will open new worlds to you. Worlds you have never experienced before."

As Tom stared at the *David*, he recounted: "Everyone has an angel inside. Follow your passion. Develop your self-confidence. And finally—for now—the beauty is in the details."

"You are an excellent student. One of the best I have ever had."

Thomas remembered the words of the guard. There had been many "students" before him. He wondered who this old man was and how he could spend his days roaming the city helping wayward souls.

"Are you ready for the next lesson, Thomas?" The question jolted Tom back to the moment.

"Yes, of course. Let's go." He turned his back on the statue and began walking toward the entrance.

5

YOUR HAND CREATES WHAT YOUR MIND CONCEIVES

*Our worlds are created through the synchronization
of the creative brilliance of the mind and
the diligent steadiness and skill of the hand.*

But the old man held him back.

"Not quite yet. There is one last lesson here before we leave. Do you remember what I said we would get to in a moment?"

"Oh yeah, you said that usually Michelangelo

wanted his statues to look lifelike—but with a few exceptions, right?"

"Correct. Now, look closely again at *Il Gigante*. What two parts of the body are out of proportion?"

"Well, the head, obviously."

"Yes. And what else?"

Tom looked up and down the statue. He saw it. "The hands! The head and the hands." Then he repeated it for emphasis, and because he was excited that he saw it. "The head and the hands."

"That is it, Thomas. Now the important question: Why?"

"I have no idea."

"I will tell you. First, there was a practical reason why the head was so large. Michelangelo knew that the head of *Il Gigante* would be some twenty feet off the ground. Of course, the farther away an object is, the smaller it appears. He made the head large to provide context, so it could be seen in proper proportion to the rest of the body as people looked up from the foot of the statue. There is a lesson here, but not the most important one. It is that sometimes parts of your life must be bigger than others in order to bring balance. Many people believe that we should keep everything equal, but not if you want to excel. If you want to be a great writer, you must spend more time reading and writing than you do, say, watching television. Many people desire greatness, but few realize the sacrifices you have to make to achieve it. Of course, here is an even more important lesson that Michelangelo taught us in sculpting the head and the hands larger than they should be."

"What's that?" Tom asked.

"Did you know that Michelangelo was a writer as well, Thomas?"

"No, but it doesn't surprise me."

"Indeed, he was very good. One thing Michelangelo wrote tells of his philosophy and gives us insight into why he made the hands and the head of *Il Gigante* larger than they should be. In one of his sonnets, he wrote,

The marble not yet carved can hold the form
Of every thought the greatest artist has,
And no conception ever comes to pass
Unless the hand obeys the intellect.

"Do you understand this lesson?"

"I guess that the head and the hands are both important. They have to work together?"

"In its basic premise, that is correct. Michelangelo knew that our worlds—and a statue—are created through the meeting of the creative brilliance of the mind and the diligent steadiness and skill of the hand. It is the bringing together of the power of the mind and the delicacy of the work of the hand. This is the fifth lesson, and the final one here. *You conceive your world in your mind and then create it with your hands.*"

The old man looked at his watch. "We must be going soon, so let me finish. Thomas, you can become anything you want in life. You can achieve whatever you desire. But you must make the connection between the head and the hands. Do you know what I mean?"

"Uh, not really."

"Thomas, most people live in one or the other. They either conceive of amazing things—they *dream*—but it never goes beyond that. They live only in their minds. Still others do just the opposite. They are filled with action, but not action that is well thought out. It is movement that takes them nowhere. The secret is this: *Let your mind conceive it and then let your hand create it.* True accomplishment requires both."

The old man pointed at the statue before them and continued, "As David stands facing his Goliath, he conceives in his mind what he wants to do. He sees the giant dead at his feet and his own army saved. But had he not trained by himself, slinging countless stones at trees and animals for years in obscurity, had he not been skilled enough to be able to make his hand obey his mind, the story would have ended much differently. Instead, he searches the ground and picks up five smooth stones, yet he only needs one to slay the giant. This is because his hand was trained to accomplish what his mind had decided should take place. With one demonstration of skill he launched a stone and set in motion his ascension to the throne. When the mind conceives something and the skilled hand makes it happen, you are well on your way to a powerful life. Thomas, this is the last lesson for you here. Take a good long look at David. He has been good to you today."

"Yes, he has."

"Come now, let's go. We must visit a friend of mine before we eat."

"We're eating?"

"Yes, of course. You eat, don't you? We shall see my friend and learn a few more lessons. *Then* we eat."

6

THE IMPORTANCE OF PLANNING AND PREPARATION

*The lesson is not to move too fast. Fast enough
to get where you want to be, but slow enough
to do it right the first time.*

Quickly they were out on the streets of Florence
again. And once again the old man was starting to
outpace Tom. This time, Tom decided to let pride
get the best of him and said nothing, opting instead to just hustle along, doing the best he could
to keep up with the old man. Carrying the heavy

backpack—and sweating profusely after only a few minutes—he was barely able to keep up. *This guy must have been on the Italian track team!*

In and out of the crowd they weaved. Tom did his best to keep his eye on the old man, all the while trying not to knock over any old women who might venture into his path. Then the old man stopped as abruptly as he had started. He turned, waved his hand at the door to a storefront workshop in the middle of the block, and announced, "Here we are, Thomas. Your next classroom."

The old man opened the door for Tom. A bell rang and announced their arrival, though not one person looked up from his work. "After you," he said, and Tom walked in, his eyes quickly scanning the room.

Interesting place, he thought.

There were about a half dozen people in the workshop, all of whom seemed lost in their work, and each, it seemed, working on a sculpture at a different stage of completion.

"Arturo!" the old man called out in singsong familiarity. "Arturo! Your old friend is here!"

Almost immediately a man came out through a door in the back of the workshop. He was about fifty, short, stocky, and with the same large arms that the old man had. "Yes, it is you! I could tell from your voice. It has been, what, three weeks since I last saw you?" The men embraced while Tom watched. "What brings you here today?" He looked at Tom. "Another student?"

Tom was beginning to wonder if the old man was running an unofficial school for tourists. Everybody seemed to know about the old man and his students.

"Yes, another student, you may say. And this one is particularly bright. I have brought him to see firsthand how one creates a masterpiece."

"Well, you may not see a masterpiece today," Arturo said, "but you can see how one goes about creating something from the cold, hard marble."

Tom continued to look around and realized he was actually looking forward to this. Being in the workshop was striking a chord with his creative side—a side he had neglected for so long.

"Please do not mind the dust. It is what comes with the trade," Arturo said.

"Another reason Leonardo didn't approve of sculpture," the old man interjected. "He didn't like to get dirty."

"Yes, well, you and I know the beauty of hard work, do we not?" Arturo asked the old man with a knowing look.

"Indeed we do."

Arturo invited them to walk around at their leisure. "As always, my workshop is yours. Please call me if I can help in any way."

"We certainly will," the old man replied. And with that Arturo went back to his work.

The old man looked around and took a deep breath. The workshop felt cool to Tom. There was a distinct smell to it, a combination of the elements and the sweat of many hardworking sculptors, most of whom he supposed could use a shower. There was dust everywhere and the incessant sound of chisel on marble, banging, and scraping. Each of the artists worked with a sense of focus, as though they were searching for their own angel.

The old man guided Tom over to the first table. On it was a relatively small piece of marble. It had yet to be touched with a chisel. When they got to the edge of the workstation, the old man said, "Thomas, take a look at this piece as it sits here. And look at the whole table. What do you see on the marble and on the table?"

"Well, on the marble I see lots of lines—I'm assuming that is where the cuts will be made, or whatever you call them. On the table I see the chisels, drawings, and little wooden statues. Oh, and a clay statue."

"That is right. Now, the importance of each: Creating a statue is much like creating a life. If you are going to become the person you want to become, then you will need to plan and prepare. Most people never plan for the kind of person they want to become, Thomas.

"Yet planning helps you do it right the first time. When you work with marble you don't get many chances to cut. One mistake can ruin a whole piece. That is why it is imperative to spend time planning your work. You see the drawings? Do you notice what kind of utensil they are drawn in?"

"Pencil, it looks like."

"Correct. This is because in the drawings you can always erase and start over. Once you separate a piece of marble you can't go back. You need to do it right the first time. Sometimes in life you can go back—as you are learning today. But you will find a little planning and preparation will save you years of frustration and regret. *Always* do the sketching and drawing first.

"Then," the old man continued, "you do the small sculpture. This is the 'test run,' as I believe you Americans call it. Some use wood. Some use clay. Others may even use marble, though that isn't necessary. The idea, Thomas, is to make sure you have everything down before you cut."

"That makes sense," Tom said.

"Then, and only then, you lay out what the sculpture

will look like on the actual marble. Thomas, do you know how many people never plan? They just dream. Dreaming isn't enough. It is a start, but then one must make sure that the dream is possible, or even desirable."

"Desirable?" Tom asked.

"Yes. Think of it for a moment, Thomas. Many students, maybe you included, grow up thinking some course of study and work would be interesting to them. They go to university and study. They do the intellectual work, and that is important. But then they graduate and begin the work and soon realize that they don't like it. By then, most people think that it is too late. They are already settled in, they are making money, and so they continue to do something they do not enjoy.

"Many people never draw out what they want their lives to look like. They do not create the miniature sculpture to decide if the actual sculpture is what they will want to have as a finished statue."

"I'm missing something."

"Yes, of course. Think of the teacher who always wanted to help people by teaching them, but when he gets into his career, he realizes that money means more to him than he originally thought. As a teacher he will never make much money. But now the teacher is stuck. He never gave significant thought to the fact that he would have certain desires for compensation. Now he feels he can't do anything else because of the investment in his education, or because he is too far into his career, or because he is afraid of what others will think.

"Or, for another example, a young person who wants to trade financial instruments realizes after a few years on the job that his personality cannot take the pressure involved. How much more enjoyment people would have in their lives and careers if they planned and not just studied, if they took the time to actually go and do what they thought would be fulfilling, instead of investing all of their money in learning about it."

"That's why we have internships, though, isn't it? I mean, are you saying internships are bad?"

"No, not at all. It is just that they don't give us the whole picture. They are focused snapshots. They do not show the whole reality, and thus cannot be a perfect view into whether or not a person will enjoy the work when they begin to do it for a living. Let me explain. Thomas, did you do an internship?"

"Yes."

"And you enjoyed it?"

"Yeah, it was fine."

"Was it a clear look at what your work is in reality now?"

"Well, no."

"Exactly my point. Many young people, and older people too for that matter, do not do enough planning, preparation, and investigation about what they want their lives to become. They either drift through life and allow circumstances to push them to and fro, or they make rash, ill-conceived plans, then move too quickly, realizing too late that they have made a mistake, and a very bad one at that. And it is a mistake that affects their very lives! Planning, Thomas, real planning; eliminates most of that."

"So what is the lesson for me? What can I do now?" Tom asked.

"Today you have learned many things, and you have made some discoveries about yourself. Tomorrow you will begin your trip home. Your mind and heart will be free to pursue whatever you desire. You will want to move very fast because of the excitement you feel. This is all very well and good. I encourage you to take action. Yet my advice is not to move *too fast*. Fast enough to get where you want to be, but slow enough to do it right the first time. Michelangelo had many deadlines that came with the commissions of his projects, and much of the time his pay was determined by the timeliness of his delivery."

"It helps to be the greatest sculptor who ever lived," Tom said.

"Indeed it does, Thomas, but at the time, while he was well known, he wasn't yet considered the greatest sculptor of all time. He was an artist who did all of his planning and preparation before ever taking the chisel to the marble. And this is one of the reasons he became as great as he was. Plan, Thomas, *plan*."

7

ALL ACCOMPLISHMENT STARTS WITH ONE SWIFT ACTION

Action is the beginning of accomplishment.
Without it, you have only wasted dreams
and good intentions.

As the old man finished speaking, he saw out of the corner of his eye another young man, an apprentice, who looked as if he was about to begin on a fresh piece of marble. "Excuse me," the old man said to the artist, "but are you about to begin with that?" He motioned to a small piece of marble, about three feet long.

"Yes, I am," said the artist.

"Very good. Do you mind if we watch?" He started to move over to the place where the artist was working. Tom followed.

When they reached the workbench, the young artist picked up one of the larger chisels and positioned it carefully. Then, with one swift blow, he brought the hammer down and took off a large piece of the marble.

"What will this be when you are finished with it?" the old man asked.

"I am hoping it becomes a lion," the artist said.

"It will be, and it will be beautiful," the old man said, hoping to encourage him. "It will take some detail to make it work. I hope you are good." He smiled.

"I'm pretty good," said the artist, also smiling.

"Well, continue to work. My friend and I will not bother you." With that, the old man backed up a bit and took Tom with him by tugging slightly at the elbow.

"We're moving on already?" Tom asked. "That's it?"

When they were about six feet away, the old man finally replied, "Thomas, what you just saw was one of the most simple and yet profound lessons any human being could ever learn. In fact, many people live in prisons of foregone dreams because they do not learn the lesson we just saw. Do you know what it is?"

Thomas was baffled. He couldn't think of one profound idea he had learned from watching the young apprentice take a whack at the marble. "Well, to be very honest, I can't imagine what profound lesson I just learned watching him for twenty seconds. You are going to have to tell me or I'll never get it."

"This one is so simple that many people do not see it. Yet it is extremely important. Here it is, Thomas: *Every successful endeavor begins with one swift action.*"

"That's it?" Tom still didn't get it.

"Think for a moment, Thomas. How many people have dreams deep within them?"

"Practically everyone, I guess."

"Exactly. Everyone. Now, what percentage of people actually live their dreams? Or what percentage even *pursue* their dreams?"

"Well, a lot fewer."

"In the grand scheme of things, Thomas, virtually no one pursues their dreams. Yes, they dream. In fact, I believe that we humans are born dreamers. Some even plan, or prepare. But very few ever *start*. And therein lies the problem. Thomas, you have learned much here today, and there are a few more insights I have for you. The key to your success when you get home will be whether you apply what you have learned here, or whether you write it off as the rants of a crazy old man. But here is the truth: This artist could plan and prepare for weeks, but if he doesn't pick up the hammer, aim, and then strike the marble, he will never get to that beautiful lion that I am sure resides within the stone. He must start, that is the key. Action is the beginning of accomplishment. Without it, you have only wasted dreams and good intentions."

"So why do you think most people don't start?" Tom asked.

"I think there are a number of reasons. One is that they never give their dreams enough thought to actually bring themselves to a place of action. Another reason is that they do not plan and lay out a strategy. Still another is that they are so involved in what they are currently doing that they cannot start on their dreams. For example, a man may have a dream of becoming a writer, but he makes $100,000 a year, has a company car and a nice retirement package. His wife doesn't work and the kids are in private school and taking piano lessons. So he asks himself whether or not he will quit and pursue his dream. The answer is almost always no."

"Yeah, that sounds like most people."

"But the last reason is perhaps the most powerful reason of all. That reason, Thomas, is *fear*."

"Fear? Of what?"

"Fear of anything. Fear of everything. Fear of the unknown. For example, what are you fearful of that would keep you from leaving your job and pursuing your creative side?"

"That my father would think I was an idiot. Fear that he'd be right. Fear that I'd fail."

"I thought you would say that. For most, their fear paralyzes them, and they never start. Some people are afraid of failing. Still others are afraid of not being able to provide for their families. Others are afraid of losing their reputation. There is the ubiquitous fear of change. Some are even afraid of *succeeding*."

"Succeeding? Why would anyone be afraid of succeeding?"

"They are afraid they won't be able to perform at that level, afraid of the responsibility that power and wealth may bring. Eventually they become afraid of falling from a much higher level. You know, a drop from one foot doesn't cause as much fear as a drop from twenty."

"I guess I never thought about that before."

"Fear, Thomas, is the driving factor for many who do

not take the simple step of starting. Let me ask you: What would you like to start when you get home?"

Tom thought for a moment, and then said, "Well, it's funny you mentioned piano lessons. I have always wanted to learn to play the piano. I am amazed whenever I hear someone play beautiful music."

"So why haven't you taken lessons before?"

A surprised look came across Tom's face. "I guess . . . I'm scared." He had never thought of it that way before.

"Scared of what?"

"Scared of not being talented enough to actually play well. Scared of what my dad will think of me. He thinks most musicians are sissies. I just have never wanted to deal with it."

"And so you have never started. You see, *fear*. But that is okay. Now you know this of yourself. When you get home you must take one swift action to start."

"Like what?"

"Open the phone book, pick up the phone, and make an appointment for your first lesson. Simple, isn't it? Yet whether or not you ever learn to play the piano depends on that simple step. You must look at your fears and then defeat them."

"Yes, I see," Tom conceded.

"Whether it is fear of failure, or that you're too old

to start something new, or that you're about to attempt something that has never been done before, people have all sorts of excuses for why they don't start what they should. Ultimately it all leads to inaction and a lack of accomplishment. Imagine if Michelangelo had done what those other artists had done: thought about what to do with the marble but never started. Who knows, that marble might still be sitting there today." He paused to let his messages sink in. Then he winked as he said, "And I would have no stories to teach you these lessons with!"

"And they are good lessons," Tom said. "Are there any more?"

"Yes, a few short lessons before we leave and enjoy our meal. I *am* getting hungry, so we must not spend too much time here."

"Okay, what are they?"

8

EMBRACING THE STAGES OF CHIPPING, SCULPTING, SANDING, AND POLISHING

We must go through the same progression:
Chip away what doesn't belong, sculpt our lives
and give them form through the people
we associate with and the information we take in,
allow the rough spots of our lives to be sanded
away through adversity and suffering, and then,
only then, are we ready to be polished and let our
power and beauty show in all their glory.

"Here, come to the center of the room with me." They walked toward a spot where Tom could see the whole room. "Look around. All of these sculptures are at different stages in their creation. They all have different work being done on them. Essentially, though, there are only four acts that take you from the raw material to the finished piece: chipping, sculpting, sanding, and polishing. That is the bulk of the work that is to be done."

"Okay . . . and what does that mean for me?"

"I like to think of life that way. There are times when the Supreme Artist chips away at us, other times when he is sculpting us, other times when he is sanding, and then times when he is polishing. All of these are needed to create a beautiful life, just as they are needed to create a beautiful sculpture."

"Okay, I can see that."

"The problem, Thomas, isn't whether people can see the process, but whether they can accept it. And furthermore, most important, whether they can *embrace* it."

"Embrace it?"

"Yes. *Embrace* it. You see, if we simply accept it, we are still not necessarily a willing participant in the process; that is, we are not necessarily participants with positive attitudes. That is key: a positive attitude about the process."

"Okay, so explain the four steps."

"Very well. Let's start with chipping. Every person has parts of them that simply must go. If those parts stay, you might never reveal the Angel Inside. If we are going to create a life of power and beauty, we must allow ourselves to go through the processes that chip away at all of the parts of us that hide our true selves. Yet most people do not embrace this process."

"Why?"

"Pain. People are afraid of pain. Physical pain. Emotional pain. Psychological pain. When we lose parts of ourselves, even bad parts that keep us from growing, it hurts. It hurts because we have become comfortable with our negative aspects. We have learned to compensate for them. So, rather than allow them to be chipped away at, we run away from the process. And because of that, we get stuck where we are and our Angel never comes to the surface."

"I need to think about that. I am not one who likes a lot of change, especially if I know it may take some work. I know what you mean about the fear of change and how we avoid it. I know I do that myself. I just never thought that it might be holding me back."

"Yes, give this some thought, Thomas. It is important.

There are parts of you that must be chipped away if you are to become the person you want to become, the person you are *destined* to become. If you do not allow the chipping away of the exterior, you will forever hide the Angel Inside."

The old man looked around for another artist he could use to make his next point. He spotted one, and pointed him out. "There, do you see the young man at that table wearing the blue smock?"

"Sure," Tom replied.

"He is an example of the next lesson. Do you see how he is using a different chisel from the one used to take off large portions of the marble?"

"Yes."

"He has begun the process of sculpting. This is different from chipping, in that chipping is taking off what doesn't belong while sculpting is the fine art of slowly and delicately revealing the form and beauty of the piece, the details we spoke of earlier. This is where the artist begins to transform the marble into the piece it is intended to become. There is a lesson here as well."

"I think I can guess, but tell me, what's the lesson?"

"Well, when we have allowed life and our own actions of discipline to eliminate that which hides our true inner selves, we then must actively form the life that we want to lead."

"How do you do that?"

"There are many tools for this, Thomas. The tools of a sculptor are few, but the tools for sculpting a life are many. We are a product of the things that we allow to shape and influence our lives. Everything and everyone that we interact with will shape and mold the person we become. This includes both what we choose to involve ourselves with, as well as what we choose not to involve ourselves with."

"Give me some examples," Tom requested.

"Let me start with what we choose to involve ourselves with. First and foremost are the people with whom we involve ourselves. Our business associates and our friends are people who we can choose at will. We should choose these people wisely for what they will help us become. We should seek out those who will challenge and encourage us to become the very best that we can become. The goal is to have a network of people around us who act as a springboard to a better life."

"That makes sense. What else?"

"The second is similar; it is the books that we read."

"Books?"

"Yes, books. I like to view books as a chance to converse with the author. I like to imagine that the author is speaking these ideas directly to me. I react and ask questions in my mind as I read, and this allows me to 'speak' with the author. This way I am not bound by the limitations of time and space. I can be friends with the greatest minds that walk, and have walked, the earth. I can invite them into my life to challenge my thinking, shape my life, and help me become a better person, a more successful person."

"I've never thought of it that way before. All those years I hated reading in school!"

"Yes, many people view reading books as boring and a waste of time, yet if they were to view it as an opportunity to sit down with the author and learn from him, they would open themselves to whole new levels of learning and growth. The lesson here, Thomas, is that our lives are sculpted and formed primarily by the people we associate with and the books we read. When people grasp that concept, they are prepared to shape their lives into what they want them to become. You understand, yes?"

"I do. Come to think of it, there are a few people who come to mind whom I really respect—and they are all readers. One even claimed that you 'can't be a leader unless you are a reader." You've convinced me to get some good books when I get home and 'make friends' with some people I've never met before, people who will make me better."

"This is good. One more piece of advice on the reading of books. I want to encourage you to spend most of your time reading the works of men and women who have passed on long ago."

"You mean dead guys?"

"Well, I wouldn't have described them that way, but yes, that is exactly what I mean."

"Why?"

"It is not because of the people themselves, but because if their books are still touching and helping people, their ideas must be lasting, and what you are looking for are ideas that have passed the test of time. You should look for *timeless* content, not *vogue* content."

"Yeah, that makes sense. I haven't read many classics lately."

"Now you will," said the old man as he turned to find another artist at another table. When he saw what he was looking for, he again redirected Tom's attention: "Can you tell what that young man is doing?"

"Well, it looks like he's sanding the statue. What is it, a cherub?"

"That is what it looks like from here. And yes, he is sanding it. Do you know what sanding represents in life, Thomas?"

"When you are being worn down?" he guessed.

"That's close. In a sense it is when we are worn down. But it is much more positive than that. Sanding represents those times in our lives when *seemingly* negative circumstances surround us. It is when things grate against us. They can be irritable if we let them be. People . . . circumstances . . . they all perform the act of sanding."

"So what is positive in that?"

"Again, most people seek comfort in their lives. They avoid suffering and adversity. Yet almost all people of significance and accomplishment have experienced tremendous adversity or suffering in their past. Those times of suffering are what give us substance, and our lives meaning. Those trials are what keep us humble and appreciative when we finally succeed. They keep us from seeking simple answers about life, because there are none. As one ancient writer told us, 'Trials produce perseverance, perseverance, character, and character, hope.' Wisdom indeed. Yet most people run from adversity, and as a result they never learn to persevere. Instead they learn to quit or hide. And there is no power in that, is there, Thomas?"

"No."

"Trials, adversity, and suffering—sanding, if you will—are all an important process in shaping our lives . . . if we handle them correctly."

"What do you mean by 'correctly'?"

"There are several ways to make sure we handle difficult times correctly. One is to accept that these trials are a part of life and to embrace them. Another is to have a good attitude about life, even when things are not going well. A third is to seek to learn from the situations, about ourselves, about the world, about life, and about people. And last, we must find the opportunity in negative circumstances. Every negative situation can bring a positive outcome if we look for it. Those who are successful are those who can turn adversity into achievement. Give that some thought as well, young Thomas."

"I certainly will."

The old man had already spotted another person he wanted to point out, and he directed Tom's eyes there. "Of course you can see what this young lady is doing."

"I am assuming from the shine she's putting on that marble that you are talking about polishing."

"Correct. Polishing—the final step. The one that represents the part of life that everyone wants to skip to."

"What's that?"

"Polishing represents the part of life that makes us look good. It is when we let the world see how beautiful we are. It is when we get to 'shine,' so to speak. It is when our Angel stands before the earth in its full glory—when we are seen by the world around us in all of our beauty and power. Everyone loves those times, don't they?"

"Well, they beat a sharp stick in the eye, that's for sure!"

The old man looked at Tom quizzically. He obviously had never heard that saying before. Sensing that, Tom added, "You know, it beats the bad times."

"Yes, of course. The polishing is certainly the enjoyable part. It is what gives us our finish. But the lesson here is that the polishing must come last. Michelangelo would have created nothing had he just started polishing that marble. First he had to chip, sculpt, and sand. Only then could he begin to polish *Il Gigante*, thus leaving the world with his lasting work of power and beauty. The same is true with life, Thomas. We must go through the same progression: Chip away what doesn't belong, sculpt our lives and give them form through the people we associate with and the information we take in, allow the rough spots of our lives to be sanded away through adversity and suffering, and then, only then, are we ready to be polished and let our power and beauty show in all their glory."

"So does that mean we can't accomplish much when we're young?"

"You have brought up a brilliant exception to my point. You should not wait until the final days of your life to shine, though most people accomplish their most significant work later on in life and make their greatest contributions then. You will find many times in your life to shine, but the point is that they will always come after the other work has been done first."

Tom stared at a nearby block of marble. "What are you thinking, Thomas?" the old man asked.

"I am just feeling a little overwhelmed with all of the information. It is all great . . . it's just so much."

"I know, Thomas. Your mind will remember what it needs to. Then when you get home, remind yourself every day so you can learn and apply these lessons slowly as you go."

"That's a good idea."

"Yes, it is. As is the idea to get dinner! Are you ready for some of Italy's finest cuisine?"

Thomas realized that he really was hungry. "I sure am! And I'll bet you know a good place."

"I know a haunt or two," the old man said with a

smile. "Let's go." With that, they both turned to leave. As they walked out the door, the old man turned inside again. "Good-bye, Arturo, my friend! I will see you soon!" Without waiting for an answer, they both walked out the door.

9

BEING CONTENT: SOMETIMES SUCCESS TAKES YEARS

Sometimes success takes years.
It takes methodical action over time.

The old man turned left as they exited and began to walk down the sidewalk. This time, however, he was going at a much slower pace. That suited Tom just fine. The old man seemed to be preparing himself for a leisurely dinner as they walked to the restaurant. He was talkative and pointed out different places of interest.

They had been walking about ten minutes when they arrived at the restaurant. It was a small place, with only ten or twelve tables. Some of the tables were set up alfresco, as the Italians enjoy in the warm weather. There was a large chalkboard just to the left of the door with a menu on it. They stopped and read it.

"Come, let's sit down. I will order for us," the old man declared. "That is, if you don't mind. I am pretty good at this."

"No. Certainly. If you like it, I am sure I will too."

The old man caught the eye of the server and pointed to one of the tables on the small terrace. The server nodded and Tom and the old man sat down.

Soon the server brought some bread and olive oil for them to start with. "Would you like water this evening?" he asked.

"Yes, by all means. One bottle."

"Very good. Do you have any questions about the menu?"

"No, I believe we are fine."

"I will be right back then."

Tom and the old man leaned back in their chairs and enjoyed the warmth of the setting sun.

The waiter returned. "What would you like this evening?"

"I will order for the both of us," the old man said. "We would like to start with a carafe of the house red."

"Yes, sir."

"And for dinner, *primi*, do you have a risotto?"

"Certainly."

"Excellent. We will have that and a formaggio gnocchi. *Secondi*, what would you recommend?"

"We have a very good fresh halibut with asparagus in a light wine sauce."

"That sounds delicious. We'll have that. And for *piatto principale*, I am hoping you have lamb with Parmesan and eggs."

"That we do."

"That sounds perfect. And of course your selection of fruit and cheese. And maybe, just maybe, we will indulge in *dolce*. But we will decide on that later."

"Thank you," said the waiter before leaving them to themselves.

"It sounds like you ordered for an army," Tom said.

"An army of two," replied the old man.

The server brought the carafe of wine and after he

had poured two glasses, the old man raised his glass for a toast. "To all you have learned today. *May it change your life forever!*" He and Tom clinked glasses and took their first sip.

"Very good," Tom said.

"Yes, I like this trattoria very much."

For the next ten minutes or so, the old man peppered Tom with questions about the other legs of his trip, hearing all about the places he had visited. Tom was somewhat excited because of all he had been able to experience, but still, in the back of his mind, he was disappointed that the other places hadn't helped him find the answers he'd come looking for. At least he was glad that he had found the old man—or had the old man found him? In any case, he was grateful for the lessons he was learning. They were simple but profound, and just what he needed to hear at this stage in his life, even if he was a little nervous and apprehensive about putting them into action.

Soon the first course was brought to the table.

Tom dug in with vigor. He hadn't realized how hungry he was. In order to save money on his trip, he had eaten less than the best cuisine. The smell in the restaurant had been overwhelming as he waited for his food to arrive. So when it did, he wasted no time diving in.

"How does it taste?" the old man asked after Tom had had a few bites. "Is it up to your standards?"

"Mmmm. Absolutely."

"You look like you haven't eaten in a week."

"If you're talking about food this good, I haven't. Two weeks actually!"

"Well, enjoy. This is my treat, you know."

"Thank you very much. I intend to take full advantage of it," Tom said with a smile.

"I normally don't like to be taken advantage of, but it is acceptable this time." With that, the old man lifted his glass of wine again and held it toward Tom. Tom recipro-cated, and the old man said, "To your coming success," as they touched their glasses together.

"So, what is the next lesson?" Tom asked.

"You are an eager learner, indeed."

"Well, time is short."

"Very well, we should begin then."

"What's the first lesson of the dinner hour?" Tom asked.

"Thomas, let me ask you: Where do you *think* you should be by now, as far as your career is concerned?"

"Well, I think that I should be making almost twice as much money, and be at least two levels above where I am in the organizational chart."

"Really?"

"Yes. Why?"

"Because that seems unreasonable."

"Why is that unreasonable? I read about people all the time who have risen much more quickly than I have at the same age."

"It is unreasonable for two reasons. First, because you've realized your current job does not engage your passions. How can you excel at what you do if you have no joy for what you do? Second, because you are placing unrealistic expectations on yourself. Which brings us to a point I must address. Yes, the media focuses on the very successful, but have you ever asked yourself what percentage they represent of the overall population? What percentage of thirty-year-olds like yourself are directors of corporations making one hundred and twenty-five thousand dollars a year?" He paused briefly and then continued. "Thomas, it is minuscule. Of course, the media must cover them. A magazine article on a thirty-year-old making twenty thousand dollars a year and stuck in the middle of the pack is hardly inspiring."

"True."

"So here is the lesson: *Sometimes success takes years.* And sometimes years and years. *Il Gigante* is thirteen and a half feet tall. As I mentioned, it took Michelangelo twenty-eight months to sculpt the statue from start to finish. That is less than six inches per *month* or less than one and a half inches per *week*. Michelangelo's successful completion of the *David* was slow any way you look at it. Yet he knew that the time and patience would be well worth the wait. Life is also like that. Sometimes success just takes years. It takes methodical action over time."

"But . . ." Tom tried to say something.

"There are no buts, Thomas! I lovingly say to you that you place too much pressure on yourself to succeed. You are telling yourself that you should be far more ahead of where you are. That just isn't true."

"But life is short. You have to get it while you can."

The server quietly set the next part of the meal before them, as he would the rest of the evening. The old man waited to speak until after the server had left the table.

"Yes, life is short. Remember, you are talking to an old man. I am older than you could possibly imagine, and yet I know that life must be paced. There are seasons to life. There is a season to build the home and a season to live in it. There is a season to tend to the crops and a season to bring them in and eat them. There are seasons of life, Thomas, and for you it is still spring. You will arrive at winter before you know it. And when you do, you will most likely long for your youth. The earlier we are in our lives the more we hope for the latter stages, and the later we are in life, the more we long for earlier times. The key is to enjoy each stage while you are in it and understand that success takes time."

"So what do I do?" Tom asked.

"Again, first you find your passion. What is it that you love? What work will bring you joy as you perform it? That is the key. People who are passionate are people who move the world and make a difference. Then, when you have found that which you are passionate about, you must give yourself time."

"You keep saying that, but why does it take time?"

"Thomas, that is life. Yes, there are the exceptions, but for most, life unfolds—careers unfold—slowly and over time. Every stage is a proving ground. Only after we have mastered each stage are we given the opportunity to move forward. It takes time at each stage to build a foundation for future success, to learn the lessons that we must learn and to develop the skills that we will need for the future. All the while, however, we are passionately pursuing what we love and preparing ourselves for greatness in the years to come."

"Okay, so how do I get over the thoughts that I have about where I am?"

"That is a fair question. I will do my best to answer.

Thomas, I find the human mind to be fascinating. It is an incredible work of art in and of itself. The amazing potential of the mind is that we can shape what we will become and believe."

"How so?"

"By what we think about. The secret is, we think about what we tend to think about. If we think about how hard things are, then we tend to worry about how hard things are. If we focus on being grateful for our lives and what we have, our thoughts will tend to be thoughts of gratitude."

"Okay, so how does that apply to me and the fact that I am disappointed in what I have achieved?"

"Imagine: Do you think Michelangelo stopped every day after completing another portion of the *David* and said to himself, 'I will never get this done. I should be further along'? Or do you think that he kept in the forefront of his mind that little by little he was completing his masterpiece and soon enough it would be done?"

"That makes sense. So what should I think?"

"What do *you* think you should think?"

"That I should enjoy where I am. That I should take the time I need to learn what I will need for the next stage of my life. That I will get to that stage soon. Is that a good start?"

"It's as good of a start as I think you can make. When you get home, begin to tell yourself these things each day. Set aside time each day to make those statements to yourself. In doing so, over time, you will reshape your thoughts to become the thoughts you desire."

10

NO ONE STARTS WITH THE SISTINE CHAPEL

Live your life and do your work
in the embodiment of excellence, and opportunities
will flow your way. People cannot, they will not,
turn an eye away from excellence.

"The next lesson is my final lesson—a lesson similar to the one that you just learned. Here it is: *No one starts with the Sistine Chapel.*"

"Catchy title."

"Thank you," the old man said with an accompanying wink. "But let me tell you what I mean by that. Many young people like yourself, and even anyone at the beginning stages of a new venture for that matter, pressure themselves to produce tremendous results as soon as they start."

"Shouldn't they?"

"Life isn't like that, Thomas. In theory it should work, but in reality . . . it rarely does. Let me give you the example from the life of Michelangelo. You see, Michelangelo, while being known for painting the Sistine Chapel, certainly didn't start with that. No, there were three pieces of work that he did over a period of years before this that brought him, one by one, to higher and higher steps of achievement, culminating in his work on the Sistine Chapel. When he was seventeen, Michelangelo did a low-relief project in marble called the *Battle of the Centaurs*. This is what put Michelangelo on the map, so to speak. It was a phenomenal work for anyone, let alone a seventeen-year-old. So he achieved something as a young man, but more was certainly to come."

"What was his next big thing?"

"His 'next big thing' was what I believe to be not only Michelangelo's most magnificent work, but the greatest sculpture ever done."

"Really? What was it?"

"It is called the *Pietà*. Do you know it?"

"Hmmm. It sounds vaguely familiar."

"Some would argue that two other statues were the next big things, and of course they were very good, but I see the *Pietà* as the next monumental piece in Michelangelo's history."

"What were the other two?"

"Oh, yes. The first was *Saint Proculus*. The second was *Bacchus*. Both are wonderfully done, but the *Pietà* ..." The old man closed his eyes, obviously picturing the sculpture in his mind and savoring its beauty.

"That good, huh?"

The old man opened his eyes. "The *Pietà* is simply stunning. Did you go to St. Peter's in Rome?"

"No. I skipped that."

"Unfortunate. You will have to come back someday and bring someone with you. Everyone should see the *Pietà*."

"You have me intrigued. What is it?"

"The *Pietà* is breathtaking. I can barely describe it, and I know it as well as anyone. Nothing I can say would do justice to the beauty of the work. It is a sculpture of Mary, seated, with the dead Christ lying across her lap. She gazes down at her dead son. It is moving, disturbing, "haunting . . . and yet inspiring. Yes, you must see it some-day, Thomas."

"Well, now I will. I wish I could go back, from the way you describe it."

The old man quickly turned back to the original topic. "Number three. Can you guess what that was?"

"It must be the *David*," Tom stated more than asked.

"Correct. And of course number four was the Sistine Chapel, the most dramatic painting ever accomplished. It is better than anything Leonardo did, I believe. There are a few important lessons to be learned from this bit of history, Thomas."

"For example?"

"As I said, *no one starts with the Sistine Chapel*. No, most people cannot accomplish their masterpieces until they have gone through the process of growing and learning from their experiences. Of course, there are a few exceptions, but for the vast majority of people, their life work is a process and a progress."

"What do you mean by a 'progress'?"

"I mean that young people, while they can do wonderful work—and they bring so much energy and vigor—must go through the process of life and experience. They must become accomplished. They must achieve the excellence at each stage of their lives that will propel them to the next stage. They must meet the people who will open doors for them and help them produce their work of beauty and power. Many young people, and I think you as well, are too impatient to feel comfortable allowing their lives to unfold. You will soon learn the brevity of life, Thomas. But there is another lesson here."

"What is it?"

"Whatever you have as your work, do it with excellence. Excellence is what will open the door for further opportunity. Many young people want opportunity, but here is a secret for the ages: Live your life and do your work in the embodiment of excellence, and opportunities will flow your way. People cannot, they will not, turn an eye away from excellence."

"So how do I do that, I mean, practically speaking?"

"The first thing is to live in the moment. Yes, we should dream. We should have visions of what lies ahead for us. But what will take us there is not the dream, but the excellence we demonstrate each and every day. It is the excellence we display in our work that will stand the test of time. The excellence in our relationships will pay its dividends later on in life when someone we met and were kind to returns the favor and gives us an opportunity that we may not otherwise have had. It is excellence in our character that will provide us the foundation of a life well lived in every area. In the end, we will reflect back on our lives as people who are deeply satisfied not only in what we have accomplished, but even more important, in what we have become. A person with accomplishments, but without an accomplished character, has not lived a life of accomplishment. Do you understand?"

"I think I do."

"Enjoy yourself now. Live your life with excellence. Become a person whom others will be proud to know. Do the best you can at your work. Above all, be passionate about what you do and how you live your life. First, yes, you will have to do some soul-searching about what it is that you are passionate about, but if you search you will find it. When you do, pursue it with your whole heart. Throw yourself into the work that you love. Do the same in your life and your relationships. A passionate life is a fulfilled life. And if you will do these things, everything that is destined to come to pass will indeed come to pass."

"I hope so."

"It will be so, Thomas. I know these things. People can change. Believe it or not, I used to have a reputation for being somewhat of a curmudgeon, but I learned some things about people . . . and I changed. You have a tremendous future ahead of you."

"Well, thanks. Let me ask you: What did you used to do? For work, I mean."

"What do you think?"

"I'm guessing sculpture."

"You guess right. How did you know?"

"By your understanding of art, obviously. But what made me sure of it was seeing Arturo's arms and noticing the similarity to yours. That is what made me think sculpture." The old man just smiled. "So, do you still sculpt?"

"No, I am retired. Now I just teach my informal students such as yourself."

"So what did you do? What did you sculpt?"

"Oh, various things, statues and reliefs. The typical. I painted a little here and there. I was a good painter, but it was working with marble that I loved the most."

"Just like Michelangelo."

"Yes, exactly like Michelangelo."

With the lessons out of the way, Tom and the old man spent the balance of their time together talking about Italy, the old man playing the part of virtual tour guide and historian. Tom found it all fascinating. When they were through with their delicious dinner, they got up and walked to the sidewalk.

"Thomas, meet me in the morning before you go so I can see you off."

"Sure, I would like that. I need to leave shortly after six, so we could meet at six."

"That would be fine. There is a large plaza on the north side of your hotel. I can meet you at the fountain there. Six a.m.?"

"Sharp. I'll be there, bags ready to go."

"I will see you then."

"Thanks for dinner tonight."

"It was my pleasure, Thomas. Good evening." The old man turned and disappeared into a group of people. Tom watched for a moment, even after he couldn't see the old man anymore, and then decided it was time to get to bed. Just as Tom turned to head back to his hotel, the old man tapped him on the back. He was holding a piece of paper.

"I have saved you some time. Read this when you get back to your room. And I will see you tomorrow morning." Tom took the paper and the old man turned again into the night.

After the short walk in the cool of the night, Tom arrived back in his room and opened the paper the old man had given him. On it were the lessons he had learned that day:

- Find the Angel within you.
- Follow your own passion.
- Be confident in your strength.
- The beauty is in the details.
- The hand creates what the mind conceives.
- Plan and prepare.
- Start with swift action.
- Embrace the stages of chipping, sculpting, sanding, and polishing.
- Sometimes success takes years, so be content.
- No one starts with the Sistine Chapel.

The old man really was prepared to teach someone today. As he lay in his bed drifting off to sleep, Tom finally believed that maybe today his life truly had changed forever. He began to believe that there was a person inside of him that he had yet to show to the world, a person like that Angel Inside. A person of power and beauty.

At six a.m., Thomas spied the old man walking toward him from the opposite side of the empty plaza. It was quiet; only a few shop owners were preparing to open for the day ahead by sweeping the doorways of their shops. As Tom and the old man reached each other, they shook hands.

"Good morning, young Thomas."

"Good morning to you," Tom replied.

"Today your journey begins. Where it takes you is up to you."

"Yes, I know. But with what you have shown me, I think I'm ready."

"When do you leave?"

"In just a few minutes, actually; I can't talk long." They stood alone in the plaza, looking at one another, the old man smiling and Tom with tears in the corner of his eyes. He couldn't believe what had happened to him. An old man had appeared out of nowhere and taught him perhaps the greatest lessons he had ever learned about life and happiness.

"Hey, by the way, I would like to keep in touch. Can I have your address?"

The old man looked at Tom for a moment, deciding. "Thomas, perhaps you can give me your information. A business card maybe. Then I can follow up with you. Is that all right?"

"Yeah, sure," Tom replied. He pulled out his wallet and found one, slightly bent, and handed it to the old man. "There you go. All the information is right. Be sure to get hold of me."

"Well then, Thomas, this is good-bye," the old man said.

"Yes, it is good-bye. Thank you. Thank you for everything," Tom said.

And the two embraced like a father and a son. "You are very welcome, young Thomas," the old man whispered in Tom's ear.

Tom pulled back and readied himself to leave. "I'll see you then."

"Good-bye."

Tom turned and began walking away while the old man simply watched. After just a few steps, Tom turned back. The old man was waiting.

"You know, I never even asked you your name. What *is* your name?"

"Thomas, you may call me Mr. Buonarroti."

"Okay then, Mr. Buonarroti. Good-bye." He turned to leave and started walking, but after just a few steps a thought crossed his mind. *Buonarroti. Buonarroti? That's familiar. Where have I seen that before? The plaques! That was Michelangelo's last name: Buonarroti.* He stopped in his tracks and spun back to the old man. What he saw amazed him.

He saw . . . *nothing.*

The old man—Michelangelo himself—was gone.

ANGEL INSIDE DISCUSSION GUIDE AND WORKBOOK

Find the Angel Inside You

- What do you think about the concept of the Angel Inside?

  _____

  _____

- How do you *feel* about the concept of the Angel Inside?

  _____

  _____

- In what ways have you felt "hidden" beneath the marble?

  _____

  _____

- Have you ever felt that others just can't see the "real you"?

  _____

  _____

- What areas of personal strength can you focus on to reveal the Angel Inside you?

  _____

  _____

Follow Your Own Passion

- Would you say you are following your own passion right now? Why—or why not?

  _____

  _____

- In what ways have others tried to get you to follow their vision for your life rather than letting you follow your own?

  _____

  _____

- What would happen if you began to follow your passion?

  _____

  _____

- What would you have to do or change to be able to follow your passion?

  _____

  _____

- Are you willing to take the risks necessary to create your life as you would like it to be? What are the roadblocks to following your passion?

  _____

  _____

- What would life be like for you if you were able to live out your passion and make your dream a reality?

  _____

  _____

Be Confident in Your Strength

- What are your strengths?

  _____

  _____

- How confident are you of your abilities in general?

  _____

  _____

- How confident are you when you are relying on your strengths?

  _____

  _____

- If you don't know what your strengths are, ask some friends to help you. Record their answers here:

  _____

  _____

  _____

- How can you imagine your life changing if you could more fully embrace and demonstrate your strengths?

  _____

  _____

The Beauty Is in the Details

- Would you say that you are a "detail person" by nature?

  _____

  _____

- If not, how would you rate your attention to detail?

  _____

  _____

- What do you think would happen if you could double your attention to detail?

  _____

  _____

- How can you see your work life improving if you paid more attention to the details?

  _____

  _____

- How can you see your home life improving if you paid more attention to the details?

  _____

  _____

The Hand Creates What the Mind Conceives

- How well would you say you understand and apply this concept?

  _____

  _____

- Which do you have a tendency to focus on, the work of the mind or of the hand?

  _____

  _____

- How much time do you spend conceptualizing? Can you establish a regular time to set aside for "dreaming"?

  _____

  _____

- What three specific actions can you take to implement your ideas?

  _____

  _____

  _____

Planning and Preparation

- On a scale of one to ten, how would you rate yourself on planning?

  _____

- On a scale of one to ten, how would you rate yourself on preparation?

  _____

- If you don't rate yourself very high in planning and preparation, are there any areas of your life that you plan and prepare well in? If so, why do you suppose that is?

  _____

  _____

- In what ways could you take simple steps to plan and prepare better?

  _____

  _____

- Do you have a set time each day or week that you devote to planning and preparation?

  _____

  _____

- Can you think of a time when you planned and prepared and the situation turned out great? How did that feel?

  _____

  _____

Start with Swift Action

- What would you like to achieve that you have not acted on yet?

  _____

  _____

- What in general keeps you from taking action?

  _____

  _____

- What is keeping you from taking action today or tomorrow?

  _____

  _____

- What three action steps could you take now to begin accomplishing your dream?

  _____

  _____

  _____

Embrace the Stages of Chipping,
Sculpting, Sanding, and Polishing

- What is one thing that you know you must
  remove from your life in order to allow your
  Angel Inside to shine through?

  _____

  _____

- What area of your life do you already see needs
  some sculpting?

  _____

  _____

- Are you going through any sanding right now?
  If so, what are you learning? If not, can you
  think of how you have been made better in the
  past from a time of sanding?

  _____

  _____

- When was the last time you felt like you had
  been polished and set up for people to admire?
  Have you ever felt that way? If not, how would
  it feel to be in that place?

  _____

  _____

Sometimes Success Takes Years: Be Content

- Have you ever felt like you weren't content? In hindsight, did it do you any good?

  _____

  _____

- Can you explain how we can be both ambitious and content at the same time?

  _____

  _____

- In what ways would it benefit you to be content right now?

  _____

  _____

- In what area can you see that success will come if you are content and let your life run its course?

  _____

- How can you change your thinking to help you become more content?

  _____

  _____

No One Starts with the Sistine Chapel

- What "Sistine Chapel" would you like to accomplish one day?

  _____

  _____

- What stages have you already gone through, and must you go through, in order to achieve the things that you dream of?

  _____

  _____

  _____

- Do you pursue excellence at every stage in order to give yourself the opportunity to grow to the next stage?

  _____

  _____

Final Questions

- What are the three main lessons you can personally take to heart from *The Angel Inside*?

  1. _____

  2. _____

  3. _____

- What are three actions that you can take today or this month to begin to allow your Angel Inside to shine through?

  1. _____

  2. _____

  3. _____

ACKNOWLEDGMENTS

Kyle Wilson and the staff at Chris Widener International.

Roger Scholl and Sarah Rainone at Currency Double-day.

Doris Michaels at DSM Agency.

Mark Sanborn and Charlie Jones.

Loraine Grover and Donna Johnson.

Thanks for all you have done to make *The Angel Inside* a success!

ABOUT THE AUTHOR

Chris Widener is one of the top leadership and personal development speakers and authors in the world today. For more than twenty years he has been a coach and adviser to some of the most successful men and women in the world. Chris's work has been lauded by industry icons such as John Maxwell, Brian Tracy, Jim Rohn, and Denis Waitley.

CHRIS WIDENER RESOURCES

Sign up for Chris Widener's FREE E-zine—go to www.Chris Widener.com today!

Order Chris's bestselling audio CD programs, including:
- Twelve Pillars—7 CDs
- Winning with Influence—8 CDs
- Extraordinary Leaders Series—13 CDs
- Invisible Profit Systems—1 CD

Go to www.ChrisWidener.com or call 877-929-0439.

Book Chris Widener to speak at your next event!
Want a speaker who will educate/train your group while instilling humor, excitement, and passion? Chris Widener is a prolific speaker and writer. With an engaging and versatile style, he provides life-changing principles of leadership, motivation, and success. Topics include:

- Twelve Pillars of Success
- Winning with Influence

- Leadership Rules of Engagement: Creating Fully Engaged Followers
- Leading Your Organization Through Change
- The Top Character Traits and Skills of Extraordinary Leaders
- Secrets of Motivating Others to Follow Your Leadership
- Right Now Leadership: What You Can Do Today to Become a Better Leader
- Live the Life You Have Always Dreamed of!
- Dare to Dream

For more information, contact:

Chris Widener International
and/or YourSuccessStore.com
2835 Exchange Boulevard, Suite 200 •
Southlake, TX 76092
877-929-0439 • 817-481-9260 DFW Metro •
817-442-1390 fax
www.ChrisWidener.com info@chriswidener.com

Also be sure to sign up for Chris Widener's FREE E-zine!